Yeah, I'm a Cat Lady.
(SORRY NOT SORRY!)

T0347436

KNOCK KNOCK®
LOS ANGELES, CALIFORNIA

Created and published by Knock Knock
6695 Green Valley Circle, #5167
Culver City, CA 90230
knockknockstuff.com

This book is a work of humorous nonfiction meant solely for entertainment
purposes. It is not intended to teach you anything helpful or accurate about
cats or turn you into a cat whisperer. In no event will Knock Knock be liable
to any reader for any damages, including direct, indirect, incidental, special,
consequential, or punitive, arising out of or in connection to the information
contained in this book. If we got something factually wrong, tell us so we
can correct it in subsequent editions.

ISBN: 978-168349414-0
UPC: 8-25703-50129-2

10 9 8 7 6 5 4 3 2 1

HEY, CAT LADY! YEAH, YOU!

It's trendy to be into cats these days. #Catlovers have overtaken social media like hairballs coughed up on the new rug. But you're the real deal, cat lady! Your love of cats goes way deeper than a hashtag—you've got the elaborate three-story kitty condo, vet bills, and clothes covered in cat fur to prove it. You paid the cost to be the cat-lady boss.

This book is for you! It's a celebration of your feline obsession in all its fun, fluffy glory. It embraces and honors your cat-whispering nature, because guess what? Being a cat lady isn't just hip and cool. It's actually important! Cat ladies sacrifice their time and love, caring for magnificent creatures—descended from lions and worshipped in ancient society—who eat pesky rodents, ease anxiety, and inspire amusing YouTube videos. Cat ladies help keep shelters empty, make life cuter, and remind us to stay in touch with our inner tigers. Cat ladies are missionaries for the animal kingdom itself.

So let your furry-freak flag fly. Of all the cat ladies around, you're the cat-ladiest!

SORRY NOT SORRY!

I secretly judge people who say they don't like cats. I mean, obviously they're lying.

SORRY NOT SORRY.

When I go to a party, I introduce myself to the cat before I say hello to the people. It's just good manners.

My cat never interrupts me when I'm telling a story, which makes her my favorite person to hang with.

My cat *always* interrupts me when I'm trying to work, which also makes her my favorite coworker.

OOPS, I'M FRESH OUT OF SORRY.

CAT LADY FAVORITE CAT BREEDS

Long-haired cats

Short-haired cats

Tiny cats

Big cats

Old cats

Young cats

Hairless cats

Sleepy cats

Playful cats

ALL THE CATS

My cat is better than my therapist. It makes me feel kind of sorry for my therapist. She'll never be as good as my cat.

SORRY . . . KINDA?

I can tell what my cat is thinking, and he often surprises me.

WISH I WERE SORRY, BUT . . .

When my cat stares at me, I know he is reading my thoughts. So I think of a magical catnip field, with open cans of tuna everywhere. Just to make him happy.

CAT LADY SONGS

Black Cat
Janet Jackson

Crosseyed Cat
Muddy Waters

**Everybody
Wants to Be a Cat**
The Aristocats

Eye of the Tiger
Survivor

Honky Cat
Elton John

**I'm a Different
Kind of Cat**
Eartha Kitt

Kitty Girl
RuPaul

Love Cats
The Cure

Smelly Cat
Phoebe Buffay
and the Hairballs, *Friends*

Stray Cat Strut
Stray Cats

The Year of the Cat
Al Stewart

**What's New
Pussycat?**
Tom Jones

FAVORITE
CAT LADY FLICKS

April and the Extraordinary World (2016)

The Aristocats (1970)

Cat's Eye (1985)

Cats (2019)

Keanu (2016)

Kedi (2016)

The Lion King (1994)

Puss in Boots (2011)

A Street Cat Named Bob (2016)

A Whisker Away (2020)

My cat is my role model for self-esteem. She's literally #self-care goals.

SORRY-ISH. (NOT ACTUALLY.)

Most of the time, my cat eats better food than I do.

SORRY... NOT!

I used to lint-roller my clothes before leaving the house. Then I realized: the cat people won't care, and the other people don't matter.

Of course I talk out loud to my cat. That's totally normal. Plus, he gives great advice.

I have more photos of my cat than anything else.

The amount of money
I have spent on cat toys
and climbers is obscene.
But think of the money I have
saved on entertainment.

SOWWY. *NOT SOWWY.*

My cat has a nicer bed than I do. Well, *beds*. She's got like 27.

I save my cat's whiskers.
It's not weird.
They hold magic powers.

My cats secretly enjoy
the silly nicknames
I bestow upon them.
Isn't that right,
Mr. Winkywhiskers?

ORRYSAY OTNAY ORRYSAY.

CAT LADY INSULTS

- You're great . . . for a dog person.

- If you were stuck in a tree, I would not call the fire department.

- Your voice reminds me of kitty claws on a chalkboard.

- I'd love to hang out but I promised my cat we'd watch *The Aristocats*.

- Your soul is drier than the really expensive kitty litter.

- Do I smell cat butt? Oh, it's just your breath.

- Your house reminds me of a dirty cat box, except a cat box would smell better.

- It's not you, it's my cat. She's allergic to you.

- Your haircut looks as good as the corner of the couch that my cat scratches.

- If you and I were the last feral cats on earth, we'd be . . . the last feral cats on earth.

My cat is like my shadow.
A shadow that jumps
in my lap when I'm going
to the bathroom.

Sometimes I put clothes in the dryer, just so my cat will have a warm laundry pile to lie on.

My cat could win a ribbon
in mouse-wrangling
at the Kitty Rodeo.

JUST OVER HERE NOT SAYING SORRY—SORRY!

I secretly love it
when people give me
cat themed gifts.
OK, not so secretly.

○ SORRY ⊗ NOT SORRY

I prefer hanging out with my cat more than humans. Sometimes. Most of the time.

#SORRYNOTSORRY

Kitten Showers should be a thing. I mean, I've been to enough baby showers.

Yes, I know my cat's astrological sign. That's how I know we're really compatible.

SORRY... KINDA?

. . . And yes, I do read his horoscope.

WISH I WERE SORRY, BUT . . .

I celebrate my cat's birthday. And if you and I are friends, *you* will too.

OOPS, I'M FRESH OUT OF SORRY.

**Personal Motto:
Ask Me About My Cat!**

SORRY-ISH. (NOT ACTUALLY.)

CAT LADY
COMPLIMENTS

- You are the only person I'd ever trust to cat-sit for me.

- You're more entertaining than a cat dancer and a laser pointer combined.

- I wouldn't mind if you shed all over my favorite black coat.

- You make me want to settle down and adopt some kittens together.

- Your friendship is like catnip for my soul.

- I hope people have nine lives too, because one lifetime with you just isn't enough.

- I would learn how to cook fish for you.

- After my cat, I love talking to you the most.

- You're sleeker than a puma, more fashionable than a leopard, fiercer than a tiger, and almost as lovable as a housecat.

- You're so charming, you could make Grumpy Cat purr.

- The only thing cuter than my cat is you.

- If we were cats, I would groom you.

- There's no one I would rather sleep in a sunbeam with.

- I like you so much, I may name my next cat after you.

- Is that a lint roller in your pants or are you just glad to see me?

- The only way I could possibly love you more is if you were a cat.

- Even Garfield would want to spend his Mondays with you.

- You + me + binge-watching cat videos = best night-in ever.

- When I'm with you my heart is a feather on a string. Tied to a stick. With like a little tiny bell.

- Home is with you . . . and my cat.

I have commissioned
a portrait of my cat.
More than once.

SORRY/NOT SORRY

I play fishtank videos
for my cat when I leave
the house so he won't notice
I'm gone.

I call my cat my baby.
Got a problem with that?

YEAH, NOPE. STILL NOT SORRY.

If I find out a potential suitor is allergic to cats?
#dealbreaker
#bye
#leftswipe

SORRY TO SAY I'M NOT SORRY!

. . . But to be honest, being allergic to cats is no excuse for not liking cats. That's what allergy medicine is for.

Yes, I'm bilingual.
I speak fluent Cat.
Meow?
Meow!

I GOTTA BE ME! SORRY . . . 'NUF SAID.

My cat is better than all the other cats. And believe me, all the other cats are **FABULOUS**.

THIS IS ME SAYIN' NOT SORRY—JUST SAYIN' . . .

PUNNY CAT NAMES

Cat Benatar

Cindy Clawford

Claw-milla Parkpurr Bowles

Ferris Mewller

Kittey Purry

Martin Luther Kitten Jr.

Pawl McCatney

Queen Catifah

Ruth Bader Ginspurrg

Sir Isaac Mewton

I actually kinda like the smell of my cat's morning breath.

SORRY/NOT SORRY

My cat thinks I'm perfect.
For a human.

FAMOUS CAT LADIES & CAT DUDES OF HISTORY

Eartha Kitt	Margaret Cho
Edward Gorey	Martha Stewart
Halle Berry	Morrissey
Kesha	Taylor Swift
Margaret Atwood	T. S. Eliot

You see cat fur.
I see love fluff.

IS IT WEIRD THAT I'M SUPER NOT SORRY?

I sometimes brush
my cat's fur more
than I brush my own hair.

SORRY NOT SORRY.

My cat has her own
social media accounts.

. . . And more followers than me.

○ SORRY ⊗ NOT SORRY

I buy snacks for myself
that I can share with my cat.
We're cute like that.

When my cat makes biscuits on me, I consider it a free massage.

SORRY. BUT NOT REALLY.

CAT LADY CARTOON CUTIES

Catbus *(My Neighbor Totoro)*

Felix the Cat

Garfield

Hello Kitty

Hobbes *(Calvin and Hobbes)*

Pusheen

Simba *(The Lion King)*

Stimpy *(Ren & Stimpy)*

The Cheshire Cat *(Alice in Wonderland)*

Tigger *(Winnie the Pooh)*

People say cats are antisocial. I say people are overly familiar.

OOPS, I'M FRESH OUT OF SORRY.

People say cats are aloof.
I say dogs are desperate
for approval.

SORRY . . . KINDA?

People say cats are snobby. I say they are self-possessed

People say cats are lazy. I say they are very busy sleeping, looking out the window, and sleeping some more.

Some people think my living room looks like a giant kitty condominium/obstacle course. That's because it is.

YEAH, NOPE. STILL NOT SORRY.

It's not weird that I have a kitty-cam so I can watch my cat sleep while I'm out of the house. Right?

CAT LADY DREAM JOBS

- Hello Kitty Brand Ambassador

- "Ugly" Cat Sweater Designer

- Cat Tree Creator

- Cat Behaviorist/Cat Whisperer

- Egyptian Queen

- Momager for Internet Famous Cat

- Cat Rescue Owner

- Cat Café Boss

- Catnip Grower/Dealer

CATNIP

- **Lost Cat Detective**
- **Cat Photographer**
- **Cat Portrait Painter**
- **Cat Groomer to the Stars**
- **Writer for *Cat Fancy***
- **CFA International Cat Show Judge**
- **Cat Massage Therapist**
- **Hollywood Cat Trainer**
- **Best Cat Sitter Ever**
- **Cat Toy Inventor**
- **Stay-at-Home Cat Mom/Dad**

If my cat wants to
lie down in the same spot
where I'm sitting, I'm happy
to make room.

SORRY... NOT!

My cat goes to the dentist and doctor more than I do.

When I go on vacation, I always bring presents home for my cat.

REAL TALK: NOT SORRY AT ALL.

CAT LADY DREAM DESTINATIONS

Aoshima Cat Island (Japan)

The Cat Boat (Netherlands)

Ernest Hemingway Home and Museum (Florida)

Hello Kitty Theme Park (Japan)

Festival of Cats (Belgium)

Kuching Cat City (Malaysia)

Lucky Cat Museum (Ohio)

Stray Cat Hostel (Turkey)

Torre Argentina Cat Sanctuary (Italy)

York Cat Trail (England)

If I have to look at pictures of your kid, you have to watch videos of my cat.

I GOTTA BE ME! SORRY . . . 'NUF SAID.

If I have to hear a story about your dumb dog, you have to hear about my fascinating cat.

ORRYSAY OTNAY ORRYSAY.

Every day is Caturday in my home.

CATURDAY PROJECTS

Bake cat-shaped cookies	Build a cat diorama	Design a fancy cat tree	DIY spa day for you & your cat
Do cat-themed puzzles	Family photoshoot with your cat	Make hand-crafted cat toys	
Make homemade cat treats		Plant a catnip garden	Sew outfits for your cat

I sometimes wish I could text my cat pictures of things I think she would like when I'm out and about.

REAL TALK: NOT SORRY AT ALL.

CAT LADY HALLOWEEN COSTUMES

- **Cat scratching post**

- **Cat Woman**

- **Cat-a-corn**
  (half cat, half unicorn)

- **Leo**

- **Lint roller**

- **Lioness**

- **Sabrina
  the Teenage Witch**

- **Tigger**

- **Veterinarian**

- **Yarn basket**

I worry that my cat knows when I've hung out with another cat and will be jealous.

When people ask if I'm a cat person or a dog person, I say I love all animals. But I'm totally rolling my eyes.

JUST OVER HERE NOT SAYING SORRY—SORRY!

I drink my tea out of a mug with my cat's face on it.

SORRY. BUT NOT REALLY.

I have turned down exciting travel opportunities because I couldn't find anyone good enough to cat-sit for me.

○ SORRY ⊗ NOT SORRY

... And apparently they don't allow cats to come on cruises. (What the ... ??)

SORRY NOT SORRY.

Don't make me choose
between you and my cat.
I will always choose my cat.

WISH I WERE SORRY, BUT . . .

Not liking cats is a deal-breaker for me. And that's not just for people I'm dating. It's for people I'm related to.

CAT LADY LIBRARY

Alice's Adventures in Wonderland .... Lewis Carroll

Angus, Thongs and Full-Frontal Snogging .... Louise Rennison

Breakfast at Tiffany's .... Truman Capote

Calvin and Hobbes .... Bill Watterson

Crazy Cat Lady .... Ester Scholten

Furmidable Foes .... Rita Mae Brown & Sneaky Pie Brown

How To Tell if Your Cat is Plotting to Kill You .... The Oatmeal

Life of Pi .... Yann Martel

The Cat Who Could Read Backwards .... Lilian Jackson Braun

The Cat Who Saved Books .... Sosuke Natsukawa

You see cat litter, I see a private kitty beach. Where they can go to the bathroom.

CAT LADY INFLUENCERS

Colonel Meow

Grumpy Cat

Hamilton the Hipster Cat

Henri the Philosopher Chat Noir

Keyboard Cat

Lil Bub

Maru

Nala Cat

OwlKitty

Venus the Two Face Cat

I don't really feel like I "own" my cat. More like the opposite, tbh.

If you want to meet me for coffee, we'll have to go to the cat café.

SORRY-ISH. (NOT ACTUALLY.)

CAT LADY POEMS

"Black Cat" —Rainer Maria Rilke

"The Cat and the Moon" —W. B. Yeats

"Cat's Dream" —Pablo Neruda

"February" —Margaret Atwood

"The Lost Cat" —Shel Silverstein

"The Naming of Cats" —T. S. Eliot

"The Owl and the Pussycat" —Edward Lear

"She sights a Bird-she chuckles-" —Emily Dickinson

"Tame Cat" —Ezra Pound

"To Mrs. Reynolds' Cat" —John Keats

CAT LADY SONGS DEEP CUTS

"Black Cat"
Ziggy Marley

"50 Something Cats"
deadmau5

"Cat Size"
Suzi Quatro

"Cool for Cats"
Squeeze

"I Am a Cat"
Shonen Knife

"Like a Cat"
Cyndi Lauper

"Lion of Love"
Alexander Lemtov,
Eurovision Song Contest

"Phenomenal Cat"
The Kinks

"Pussycat-Meow"
Deee-Lite

"Wildcat"
Ratatat

People say "crazy cat lady" like it's a bad thing.
I don't get it.

SORRY... NOT!

My cat and I both love sushi. Actually, she was the one that got me into it.

I have a list
of names for future cats.
I update it often.

I was a cat lady before being a cat lady was cool.

MOST PURRFECT CAT PUNS EVER

I love you—meow and forever.

You've cat to be kitten meow!

You never fur-get your first cat!

Meow ya doing? I'm feline fine!

Your *Tiger King* costume is freaking meow out!

To me, you are purr-fect. Fur real!

Your *Puss In Boots* impression is hiss-terical!

It's a cat-astrophy when we run out of kitty treats.

Fluffy, you're pawesome—and so purrty.

Could I love my cat more? It's litter-ally impaw-sible.

**Cats are like firemen.
I've never seen an ugly one.**

My cat can have fun with a ball of tin foil. I think there's a life lesson in there for all of us.

My cat is an excellent alarm clock. Well . . . at least a warm and furry alarm clock.

ORRYSAY OTNAY ORRYSAY.

. . . She also makes a great sleeping mask.

I GOTTA BE ME! SORRY . . . 'NUF SAID.

CAT LADY ALBUMS

Cats Under the Stars
Jerry Garcia Band

Cats: Complete Original Broadway Cast Recording

Cheshire Cat
Blink-182

The Greatest
Cat Power

Mambo for Cats
Jim Flora

Only Cat People Understand
iAmMoshow

The Pink Panther
Henry Mancini

Rant N' Rave with the Stray Cats
The Stray Cats

Taming The Tiger
Joni Mitchell

The Very Best of Cat Stevens
Cat Stevens

My cat just gets me.
Like, *really* gets me.

I know I'll never fully understand my cat, but I'll always enjoy trying. Isn't that what we all want in a companion?

○ SORRY ⊗ NOT SORRY

I'm not saying cats are better than people, but . . . CATS ARE BETTER THAN PEOPLE.

SORRY NOT SORRY.

THE END